BAKE IN BLACK

MUSIC-INSPIRED BAKING

EVE & DAVID O'SULLIVAN

PHOTOGRAPHY BY STUART OVENDEN

floodgallery
publishing

Flood Gallery Publishing
3, Greenwich Quay
Clarence Road
London
SE8 3EY

www.thefloodgallery.com

First published in 2014 by Flood Gallery Publishing
Copyright 2014 Flood Gallery Publishing
Second Impression 2015
Third Impression Paperback 2017

Photography: Stuart Ovenden
Food styling: Kate Calder and Eve O'Sullivan
Prop styling: Rachel Vere
Concept and art direction: David O'Sullivan

Printed in Singapore

British Library Cataloguing in Publication Data.
A catalogue record for this book is available from the British Library.

ISBN: 978-0-9928366-1-0 HARDBACK
ISBN: 978-1-9113740-2-2 PAPERBACK

FOR OUR FAMILIES

"When we asked Eve why she started Bake in Black she replied, 'I like puns and I like buns'. Bake in Black have brought another dimension to our Classic Album Sundays events so that people not only fully immerse themselves sonically into an album, but they can taste it, too! Our attendees love the play on song titles that could only be created by die-hard music obsessives, so they are smiling before they even sample their delectable treats. And there is no better marriage than music and food!"

Colleen 'Cosmo' Murphy, Founder of Classic Album Sundays

CONTENTS

INTRODUCTION

Bake in Black started life as a blog from our humble kitchen in East London. For us, music and food are a natural partnership; one of us is a food journalist, the other a musician. The idea is simple: we take a song or an album title by a band we love, which then inspires us in our creation of a recipe. Listening to records while cooking, we aim to capture the essence of those bands to pay our tribute. As each bake takes shape, we listen to their music, soaking up what it's about, and infuse it into the food. The puns come after as we sit back with a beer looking to give our sweet creations a fitting title. Combining our passions seemed a little odd at first, but soon became a project we were telling everyone about.

Our blog documented each bake and the story behind it; reminiscing about where we'd seen a band or first listened to their music and the effect it had on us. It wasn't long before we were invited to food festivals, music events and launches, and asked to create one-offs for parties and riders. Fundamentally though, our attitude to food hasn't changed: straight up home baking with a fun twist. But why serve your doughnuts on bohemian tableware when you could get your antique Les Paul guitar or a Marshall amplifier stack involved? Although the food is presented a little differently, this book is as practical and usable as any other baking book you might pick up.

We channel the vibes of such rock lords as Alice Cooper, Metallica and Iron Maiden to invent unique recipes and present them in a way that's unconventional; food is the new rock 'n' roll after all. Bake in Black takes home bakes and gets them stage-ready for a night at the Hammersmith Apollo or comfortable at the bar in dark and sweaty CBGB's.

We have a raw enthusiasm for unique flavour combinations, twists on classics, and cooking with booze – naturally. Each one of these recipes has a story to tell, and a life of its own. The Ozzy Osbourne-inspired Chocolate Bark came to life when chatting about the first heavy metal records we ever bought, but now it's something we make for presents at Christmas. Our Nirvana cheesecake looks great adorned with a smiley face, and takes about as long to make as a listen to their classic album Bleach, but it's also not half bad with a little extra passion fruit on top for a birthday party.

We've divided the book into six chapters, by type, and the range broadly covers the hard rock music genres we've referenced. There's everything from a stadium-sized Guns n' Roses cake (page 24) – aptly named 'Sweet Tooth o' Mine' – to super-simple espresso cheesecake cups dedicated to Soundgarden (page 134), and brightly spiced scones for the love of Rainbow (page 56). The recipes are suitable for everyone, with those who love baking in mind. A full list of kitchen equipment and suppliers is at the back.

We have photographed each of the recipes to capture them in an environment that reflects their inspiration. We believe food comes to life when you think outside the box, and the pictures provide the link to the song, album artwork or band that we've paid homage to.

Over the last couple of years, whether baking for Scott Ian of Anthrax, or Scott Gorham of Thin Lizzy/Black Star Riders, we've learned that everyone enjoys a treat... and a cheeky pun!

Bake in Black – Cooking on Gas Mark 666.

BIG CAKES

NIRVANA BIG CHEESE (CAKE)

IRON MAIDEN FLOURSLAVE

SEX PISTOLS GOD SAVE THE CREAM

ALICE COOPER SCHOOL'S OUT

NINE INCH NAILS THE DOWNWARD SPIRAL

GUNS N' ROSES SWEET TOOTH O' MINE

SEPULTURA BENEATH THE REMAINS

MEGADETH MEGADETH BY CHOCOLATE

SLAYER REIGN IN RED VELVET

MAYHEM DE MYSTERIIS DOM SULTANAS

BIG CHEESE (CAKE)

Double chocolate and passion fruit cheesecake

Serves 8-10

For the base
200g double chocolate-chip cookies
50g butter, melted

For the filling
250g full-fat soft cheese
250g mascarpone
400g milk chocolate, chopped
3 passion fruit, pulp and seeds removed

To decorate
100g dark chocolate
1 tube black gel colouring
Yellow icing pen or 1 passion fruit, pulp and seeds removed, to decorate

1   Crush the cookies in a food processor or bash them up in a sealed freezer bag with a rolling pin. Tip into a mixing bowl, then pour over the melted butter and stir through until the cookie crumbs are evenly coated.

2   Press into the base of an 18cm or 20cm springform or loose-based tin, then chill in the fridge while you make the filling.

3   Mix the soft cheese with the mascarpone. Put the chopped milk chocolate in a glass bowl set over, but not in, a pan of simmering water and melt. Let it cool a little, then pour it into the cheese mixture and mix until incorporated. Spoon into the tin. Swirl the passion fruit seeds and pulp through the mix, then put in the fridge to set for about 4 hours.

4   To decorate, melt the dark chocolate in a clean bowl, using the same method as above, then add the black gel colour and mix together until black. Pour over the cheesecake, level, then return to the fridge to set for half an hour.

5   To decorate, lightly carve the Nirvana logo into the chocolate topping, then fill in with a yellow edible icing pen or top with passion fruit pulp.

FLOURSLAVE

Wholemeal and ale waffle stack cake with vanilla cheesecake ice cream and lemon caramel

Serves 8-10

For the vanilla cheesecake
ice cream
200ml condensed milk
300ml double cream
1 vanilla pod, seeds scraped
100g soft cheese
**4-6 digestive biscuits, roughly
crushed**

For the lemon caramel
400g caster sugar
Juice and zest of 2 lemons
60g butter, diced
100ml double cream

1 First, make the ice cream. Pour the condensed milk and cream into a large bowl, then stir in the vanilla seeds. Using an electric whisk, whip the cream mixture until thickened and stiff.

2 Whisk the soft cheese until light and fluffy, then spoon into the same bowl as the ice cream base and beat with a wooden spoon until combined. Scatter the digestive biscuits over, fold through the ice cream, then spoon into a lidded, freezer-proof container and freeze until firm.

3 To make the caramel, spread the sugar evenly in the base of a saucepan or frying pan, then heat gently until melted, swirling it around by moving the pan, rather than stirring it. Once golden brown, remove from the heat, add the lemon juice and zest, whisk in the butter piece by piece, and then stir in the cream until combined. Allow to cool.

Recipe continues on next page

FLOURSLAVE

Wholemeal and ale waffle stack cake with vanilla cheesecake ice cream and lemon caramel

For the waffles
250g plain flour
250g wholemeal flour
2 tbsp baking powder
1½ tsp salt
2 tbsp caster sugar
5 eggs
800ml Trooper beer
200g butter, melted

4 To make the waffles, heat a waffle maker, or put a griddle pan over a medium heat. Mix the flours, baking powder, salt and sugar in a large bowl.

5 Whisk the eggs, beer and melted butter together, then pour into the flour mix to create a batter with the consistency of double cream. Pour into the waffle maker, then cook for 3 minutes, or until golden brown and crisp. Continue to cook until all the batter is used up, keeping the cooked waffles warm in a low oven as you do.

6 To assemble the waffle stack, line up the waffles, four by four, then stack another four waffles on top. Repeat with three waffles square, then two waffles, until you are left with one waffle at the top.

7 Gently reheat the lemon caramel. Add three scoops of ice cream to the top of the pile, then drizzle with the sauce and serve with extra of both on the side.

GOD SAVE THE CREAM

Angel cake with minted whipped cream, strawberries and blueberries

Serves 8

For the cake
125g flour
300g caster sugar
10 egg whites
½ tsp salt
1 tsp cream of tartar
Zest of 1 lemon
1 tbsp lemon juice
1 tsp vanilla extract

For the topping
Large handful of mint leaves, shredded
3 tbsp caster sugar
4 tbsp water
300ml double cream
100g strawberries, to decorate
100g blueberries, to decorate

1 Preheat the oven to 180C/375F/gas mark 4. Mix ⅓ of the sugar with the flour, sift, then set aside.

2 With an electric whisk, beat the egg whites for a couple of minutes until frothy, then stir in the salt, cream of tartar, lemon zest and juice and vanilla extract, then whisk again for about 3 minutes, to stiff peaks.

3 Beat in the remaining ⅔ of sugar, a spoonful at a time, until thick and glossy. Fold in the flour and sugar mix bit by bit, as gently as possible, to keep the air in the mix.

4 Spoon into an angel cake tin, or an unbuttered 22cm round cake tin, then level the top, and bake for around 45 minutes, until a skewer inserted into the centre comes out clean. Immediately turn the tin upside down on its legs, or over a wire rack, and leave to cool for 45 minutes.

5 To make the topping, put the mint, sugar and water in a pan, bring to a boil then simmer for a couple of minutes, take off the heat and allow to cool. Strain, then set aside.

6 Whip the double cream to soft peaks, then spoon in 2 tbsp of the mint syrup, or more, to taste, then whip the cream until stiff.

7 Cover the sides and the top of the cooled cake with the minted cream, then decorate with the strawberries and blueberries. Serve immediately.

ALICE COOPER

SCHOOL'S OUT

Orange and cardamom marble cake
with strawberry buttercream

Serves 8-10

For the cake
225g unsalted butter
250g caster sugar
4 eggs
250g flour
1 tsp baking powder
Zest and juice of 1 orange
1½ tbsp ground cardamom
**2 drops of natural green gel
food colouring**

For the buttercream
**6-8 strawberries, roughly
chopped, plus extra to serve
(optional)**
300g unsalted butter, softened
600g icing sugar
**100g white fondant icing
(optional)**
**Black icing decorating pen
(optional)**

1   Heat oven to 180C/375F/gas mark 4. Butter and line a 20cm tin.
    Beat the butter and sugar together with an electric whisk until pale,
    light and fluffy. Add the eggs one at a time, beating between
    each addition. Sift the flour and baking powder together, then fold
    into the mix.

2   Divide the mixture between two bowls. Stir the orange juice and
    zest into the mixture in one of the bowls, and the ground cardamom
    and green gel colour into the other. Drop spoonfuls of each batter
    into the base of the tin alternately, one on top of the other so
    the mix gradually spreads across the base of the tin. Don't try
    to swirl the mixes at this stage, as they will gradually spread
    out by themselves.

3   Bake the cake for 35-40 minutes, or until a skewer comes
    out clean. Leave to cool on a wire rack.

4   To make the buttercream, blitz the strawberries to a puree with
    a stick blender, then set aside. In a medium-sized bowl, beat the
    butter until pale and fluffy with an electric whisk, around 2 minutes.
    Gradually add the icing sugar, then mix in the strawberry puree.

5   To assemble the cake, slice in half, then sandwich together with
    the buttercream. Use the rest to ice the sides and top of the cake,
    making sure it's evenly covered.

6   To decorate, either cover with halved strawberries, or cut the fondant
    icing into a ribbon, lay across the tip of the heart, then write a name
    of your choosing.

THE DOWNWARD SPIRAL

Walnut, coconut and chocolate
spiral bundt cake

Serves 8-10

For the cake
170g salted butter
340g caster sugar
1 tsp almond essence
3 eggs
200g self-raising flour
40g cocoa powder
A pinch of salt
300ml milk
75g milk chocolate,
roughly chopped

For the walnut and
coconut marble
50g flour
70g dark brown sugar
70g salted butter, cubed
50g shredded, sweetened
coconut
A large handful of walnuts,
finely chopped

1 First, prepare the marble. Mix the flour and the sugar, then rub the butter into the mix until it resembles fine breadcrumbs. Stir in the coconut and walnuts, then set aside.

2 Preheat the oven to 180C/375F/gas mark 4. Lightly butter the bundt tin. In a large bowl, beat the butter and sugar until combined, then add the almond essence. Beat in the eggs one at a time, until incorporated.

3 Sieve the flour with the cocoa powder and salt, then stir into the batter. Pour in the milk, stir until combined, then spoon half of it into the bundt tin.

4 Add blobs of half the walnut and coconut marble evenly in the tin. Then, using a knife, gently swirl the mixture through the chocolate cake batter – make sure you don't mix it too much, as it will ruin the marble effect. Repeat with the other half of the cake mixture and marble, then bake for 50 minutes to 1 hour, until a skewer inserted into the middle comes out clean.

5 Allow to cool in the tin for 10 minutes, then turn out onto a wire rack to cool completely. Once cool, melt the milk chocolate in a glass bowl set over, but not in, a pan of simmering water, then drizzle down the grooves of the cake, or diagonally across it.

GUNS N' ROSES

SWEET TOOTH O' MINE

Three-tier honey, molasses and maple cake
with cream cheese icing

Serves 20-25

For the honey cake
400g self-raising flour
1 tsp salt
300g butter, softened
200g dark brown sugar
4 eggs
250g runny honey

For the molasses cake
300g self-raising flour
¾ tsp salt
1 tsp mixed spice
1 tsp ground ginger
225g butter, softened
150g light brown sugar
3 eggs
150g molasses

For the maple cake
200g self-raising flour
½ tsp salt
150g butter, softened
100g caster sugar
2 eggs
150ml maple syrup

1   First, make the honey cake. Preheat the oven to 170C/350F/ gas mark 4, then butter and line one 23cm, one 20cm and one 18cm cake tin.

2   To make the honey cake, sift the flour and salt, then set aside. Beat the butter and sugar together until light and fluffy, then add the eggs, one by one. Stir in the honey, then fold in the sifted flour. Spoon into the 23cm tin, then bake for 45-50 minutes, until a skewer inserted into the centre comes out clean. Set aside to cool on a wire rack.

3   To make the molasses cake, sift the flour and the salt with the spices, then set aside. Beat the butter and sugar until light and fluffy, then beat in the eggs, one at a time. Stir in the molasses, then fold in the flour mixture. Spoon into the 20cm tin, then bake for 30-35 minutes, until a skewer inserted into the centre comes out clean. Set aside to cool on a wire rack.

4   To make the maple cake, sift the flour and salt, then set aside. Beat the butter and sugar until light and fluffy, then add the eggs, one a time, before stirring in the maple syrup. Add the flour mixture, then stir until combined. Spoon into the 18cm tin, then bake for 25 minutes, until a skewer inserted into the centre comes out clean. Set aside to cool on a wire rack.

Recipe continues on next page

SWEET TOOTH O' MINE

Three-tier honey, molasses and maple cake
with cream cheese icing

For the buttercream
500g cream cheese
250g butter
2 tsp vanilla extract
300g icing sugar

To assemble
200g flaked almonds, toasted

5 To make the buttercream, beat the cream cheese, butter and vanilla
extract with an electric whisk, until smooth, then gradually add
the icing sugar until stiff.

6 To assemble the cake, slice each type of cake in half horizontally, then
place the bottom of the honey cake on a cake stand or serving platter.
Spread with some buttercream, then top with the top of the honey cake.
Spread a little buttercream in the centre of the cake, then add the bottom
half of the molasses cake. Spread with buttercream, then sandwich with
the top half. Repeat this process with the maple cake, then cover the
tops and sides with the rest of the buttercream.

7 Decorate with belts, bandanas and roses if you like, or keep it simple
with flaked, toasted almonds.

SEPULTURA

BENEATH THE REMAINS

Brazilian 'anthill' cake with sprinkles and milk chocolate cream glaze

Serves 10-12

For the cake
200g flour
2 tsp baking powder
A pinch of salt
200g salted butter
200g caster sugar
1 tbsp vanilla bean paste
4 eggs
50g chocolate sprinkles,
or half a jar

For the glaze
200g dark chocolate,
chopped, plus extra grated,
to serve
200ml double cream
50g butter, diced

1 Preheat the oven to 180C/375F/gas mark 4, then butter and line a 20-22cm, deep cake tin. Sift the flour, baking powder and salt together, then set aside.

2 In a large bowl, beat the butter and sugar together until pale and fluffy, then add the vanilla bean paste. Add the eggs one by one, stirring to combine, then fold in the flour mixture. Stir through the chocolate sprinkles, then spoon into the tin and bake for 35-40 minutes, until a skewer inserted into the centre comes out clean. Allow to cool completely on a wire rack.

3 To make the glaze, put the chopped chocolate into a bowl, then heat the double cream in a small saucepan until just boiling and pour over the chocolate. Allow to stand for a minute, then stir until smooth. Add the butter piece by piece, stirring until incorporated.

4 To decorate, spread the glaze over the cake, allowing the glaze to drip down the sides. Scatter with extra grated chocolate, then serve.

MEGADETH BY CHOCOLATE

Chocolate and meringue death by chocolate layer cake

Serves 8

For the cake
60g 70% cocoa dark chocolate, grated
70ml water
3 eggs
100g sugar
130g plain flour
Pinch of salt

For the chocolate meringue
75g milk chocolate, chopped
3 egg whites
175g caster sugar

For the chocolate icing
2 egg whites
120g icing sugar
250g unsalted butter
150g 70% cocoa dark chocolate, plus extra for curls to decorate (optional)

1 Preheat the oven to 180C/375F/gas mark 4, then grease and line a 20cm cake tin. To make the cake, mix the chocolate and the water in a small glass bowl, then place over a pan of simmering water and stir until melted, with a consistency similar to thick cream. Set aside to cool.

2 Keeping the pan of water over the heat, mix the eggs and sugar in another glass bowl, then whisk over the simmering water, until very pale, thick and mousse-like. Take off the heat, then continue whisking for a couple of minutes, until the mix has cooled. Mix the flour and the salt, then sift over the egg mix and fold until just combined. Pour in the melted chocolate, gently folding again until just combined, then spoon into the cake tin and cook for around 35 minutes – it's done when the sponge springs back when gently pressed with your fingertip. Cool a little in the tin, then turn it out and allow to cool completely on a wire rack.

3 While the sponge is cooling, make the meringue layer. Turn the oven down to 140C/290F/gas mark 1. Line a baking tray with baking paper, then draw a 20cm circle with a pencil. Turn the sheet over, so the pencil lead is on the tray side.

4 Put the milk chocolate in a glass bowl, then melt in a pan over simmering water. Next, whisk the egg whites until stiff, around 5 minutes. Add the sugar gradually, 1 tbsp at a time, whisking between each addition until the mixture is thick and glossy, then pour in the melted chocolate and gently fold through to marble. Spread the mixture evenly on the baking paper, then cook for 1 hour, until dry and crisp. Allow to cool on a wire rack while you make the filling.

Recipe continues on next page

MEGADETH BY CHOCOLATE

Chocolate and meringue death
by chocolate layer cake

5 Put the egg whites and sugar in a glass bowl, then place over, not in, a pan filled with simmering water, beating until firm and thick, around 5 minutes, then remove from the heat. Put the chopped chocolate in a clean glass bowl, then put over the water, stirring until melted, and set aside.

6 In a separate bowl, beat the butter until light and creamy. Gradually add the butter into the egg white mixture, then, once incorporated, pour in the melted chocolate, mixing until smooth.

7 To assemble the cake, slice the cooled sponge in half, then put the bottom half on a cake stand or serving plate. Spread with the chocolate filling, then place the meringue layer on top. Spread with more chocolate filling, then top with the remaning sponge half and spread the rest of the buttercream on top. Decorate with chocolate curls, if using, then serve.

REIGN IN RED VELVET

Four-layer red velvet cake with
coconut buttercream

Serves 12

For the cake
350g flour
300g caster sugar
4 tbsp cocoa powder
1 tsp salt
1 tsp bicarbonate of soda
2 eggs, beaten
375ml vegetable oil
250ml milk or buttermilk
1 tsp vanilla extract
**3-5 drops of red gel food
colouring**

For the buttercream
200g butter
200g vegetable shortening
**200g block of creamed
coconut, grated**
750g icing sugar
**Desiccated coconut/coconut
flakes, to decorate**
**Red edible icing pen,
to decorate**

1 Heat the oven to 180C/375F/gas mark 4 then butter and line two
20cm cake tins. In a large mixing bowl, combine the dry ingredients,
then whisk together all the liquid ingredients.

2 Stir the liquid ingredients into the dry, then pour into the cake tins.
Bake for 35-40 minutes, until a skewer inserted into the centre of
each cake comes out clean. Allow the cakes to cool a little then
remove them from the pans and set on a wire rack to cool completely.
Once cooled, slice each of the cakes in half.

3 To make the buttercream, beat the butter and vegetable shortening
together with an electric whisk until light and fluffy, then add the
grated coconut and beat until combined. Gradually beat in the icing
sugar, little by little, until sweet and stiff enough to spread.

4 Sandwich the cake slices together with the buttercream, then sprinkle
the top of the cake with desiccated coconut, and gently press around
the sides of the cake. Using a toothpick or skewer, carve the Slayer
logo into the buttercream, then, using a red edible icing pen,
fill in the logo.

MAYHEM

DE MYSTERIIS DOM SULTANAS

Thyme, pear, honey and sultana cake

Serves 10-12

150g golden sultanas
150g sultanas
5 tbsp pear schnapps
200g butter, softened
200g light brown sugar
3 eggs
1 tbsp honey
200g plain flour
1 tsp baking powder
1 tsp bicarbonate of soda
2 sprigs of thyme, leaves picked and finely chopped
1 tsp mixed spice
2 conference pears, peeled and grated
300ml double cream, to serve

1   Heat the oven to 180C/375F/gas mark 4, then grease a cathedral-shaped or normal bundt tin, or line a 20cm cake tin with baking paper. In a small bowl, mix the sultanas with the schnapps, then allow to soak for 30 minutes.

2   Beat the butter and sugar together with an electric whisk until light and fluffy, then add the eggs one by one, beating to combine. Mix in the honey, then add the flour, baking powder, bicarbonate of soda, thyme, mixed spice and pears. Drain the sultanas, reserve the liquid, then stir through. Spoon into the tin and bake for 45-50 minutes, until a skewer inserted into the cake comes out clean.

3   Allow to cool for around 10 minutes in the tin, then turn out onto a wire rack to cool completely.

4   Lightly whip the double cream, then add a little of the reserved sultana schnapps liquid, to taste. Serve with the cake.

SMALL BAKES AND BROWNIES

THE CLASH ROCK THE CAKE BARS

DEEP PURPLE SMOKE ON THE ROSEWATER

AEROSMITH SWEET EMOTION

JUDAS PRIEST BAKING THE LAW

AC/DC BAKE IN BLACK

CANNIBAL CORPSE BAKED AT BIRTH

RAINBOW SINCE YOU'VE BAKED SCONES

RUSH LIMESLICE

MEAT LOAF BATTENBERG OUT OF HELL

ALICE IN CHAINS THEM BUNS

KISS I WAS MINT FOR LOVING YOU

STATUS QUO BLUEBERRY FOR YOU

THIN LIZZY WHISKEY IN THE BAR

BLACK FLAG RISE ABOVE

BLACK SABBATH FAIRY CAKES WEAR BOOTLACES

THE CLASH

ROCK THE CAKE BARS
Homemade Jaffa orange and dark chocolate cake bars

Makes 8

For the cakes
175g self-raising flour
1 tsp salt
½ tsp baking powder
Zest of 1 Jaffa orange
175g unsalted butter
175g caster sugar
2 eggs
1 tbsp milk

For the topping
½ pack orange jelly cubes
100g dark chocolate

1   Start by making the jelly mixture according to packet instructions in a shallow, square baking tin, around 20cm x 20cm. Chill in the fridge until set, around 2 hours.

2   Preheat the oven to 180C/375F/gas mark 4. Mix the flour with the salt, baking powder and orange zest, then set aside.

3   Beat the butter with the sugar until pale and fluffy, then add the eggs one by one, beating until incorporated. Sift over the flour mixture, then stir to combine, adding the milk if the mixture needs to be loosened. Spoon into mini-loaf cases, then bake for 20 minutes, until cooked through. Allow the cakes to cool.

4   While the cakes are cooling, cut the jelly into strips roughly the same size as the tops of the loaves, or slightly smaller. Melt the chocolate in a small glass bowl over, but not in, a pan of simmering water. Place a slice of orange jelly over each cake, so it just sits on top, then spoon the dark chocolate over, until the jelly is covered. Chill in the fridge until the chocolate has hardened, then peel away the loaf cases and serve.

DEEP PURPLE

SMOKE ON THE ROSEWATER

Gluten-free chocolate, almond and beetroot cakes with rosewater icing

Makes 12

For the cakes
175g ground almonds
2 tsp gluten-free baking powder
A pinch of salt
75g cocoa powder
200ml vegetable oil, plus extra for greasing
200g light brown sugar
3 eggs
Zest and juice of 1 medium orange
200g raw beetroot, peeled and finely grated

For the rosewater icing
120g icing sugar
1-2 tbsp hot water
A few drops of rosewater, to taste
2-3 drops pink food colouring (optional)

1   Preheat the oven to 180C/375F/gas mark 4. Grease a 12-hole mini-bundt tin or line a muffin tin with paper cases.

2   In a large bowl, mix the ground almonds, baking powder, salt and cocoa powder, then set aside.

3   In a small saucepan, gently warm the oil with the sugar, stirring until dissolved, then remove from the heat and allow to cool a little. Beat the eggs with the orange zest and juice, then stir into the sugar mix. Tip the grated beetroot into the dry mix, and pour the egg mix into the bowl, stirring until combined.

4   Spoon the mix into the bundt tins, then bake for 20-25 minutes, until a skewer inserted into the centre comes out clean. Allow to cool in the tin for 10 minutes, then turn out onto a wire rack and cool completely.

5   To make the icing, sift the sugar into a bowl, then add a little water at a time, until you get a cream-like consistency. Add a few drops of rosewater, tasting as you go to make sure it doesn't become overpowering, then add pink colouring, if you like. Drizzle over the bundt cakes, and allow to harden.

SWEET EMOTION

Mini Boston cream pies with vanilla custard and chocolate glaze

Makes 12

For the cakes
80g plain flour
½ tsp baking powder
A pinch of salt
3 eggs
80g caster sugar
Juice of ½ an orange

For the custard
200ml whole milk
1 vanilla pod, split lengthways and seeds removed
2 egg yolks
2 tsp caster sugar

For the glaze
100g dark chocolate, roughly chopped
75ml double cream

1   Preheat the oven to 190C/380F/gas mark 5. Butter and line a deep swiss roll tin, a 12-hole mini-cake tin (no need to line) or a 20cm x 15cm buttered and lined roasting tin. Sift the flour, baking powder and salt into a bowl, then set aside.

2   To make the cakes, crack the eggs into a large, glass bowl, whisk lightly, then add the sugar and orange juice. Put over a pan of simmering water, making sure the base doesn't touch the water. Whisk for 5 minutes, until light and fluffy and almost doubled in size. Remove from the heat, then scatter over the sifted flour mix and gently fold into the eggs with a metal spoon – you need to keep as much air in the mix as possible.

3   Spoon the mix into the tin, then bake for about 15 minutes, until golden on top. Allow to cool in the tin for 5 minutes, then turn out onto a wire rack to cool completely. If using a roasting tin or swiss roll tin, stamp out 6cm circles of cake with a biscuit cutter – you should be able to cut about 18-20 cakes. If using a mini-cake tin, slice each cake in half.

4   While the cakes are cooling, make the custard. Put the milk in a small saucepan with the vanilla pod and seeds, bring to the boil then take off the heat immediately and set aside to infuse for 15 minutes.

Recipe continues on next page

SWEET EMOTION

Mini Boston cream pies with vanilla
custard and chocolate glaze

5 Lightly whisk the eggs and sugar together, then pour the slightly
cooled milk mixture (with the vanilla pod fished out) into the mix.
Whisk together, then pour into a clean saucepan and cook over
a low heat, stirring frequently, until thickened, around 5 minutes.
Once thickened, pour into a bowl and press clingfilm over the top
of the custard to stop a skin forming. Allow to cool for 10 minutes,
then chill in the fridge.

6 Once the cakes are cool and the custard is chilled, heat the cream
for the glaze in a small saucepan, until almost boiling. Put the
chopped chocolate in a small bowl, then pour the cream over and
allow to stand for a minute. Stir until melted and glossy.

7 To assemble the cakes, spread a generous amount of cooled custard
on the base of a cake, around 1cm thick, then top with another cake.
Spread the glaze over the top of each cake, then leave to stand for
30 minutes to set. Serve, or put in the fridge until ready to eat.

BAKING THE LAW

Sugar-coated buns with rhubarb jam
and whipped cream

Makes 16

For the buns
**300ml milk, plus extra
to glaze
40g unsalted butter
500g strong white flour
1 tsp salt
7g sachet fast action yeast
1 egg, beaten**

To assemble
**100g butter, melted
100g caster sugar
8 tbsp rhubarb jam
300ml double cream,
whipped**

1   First, put the milk and butter in a small saucepan over a medium
heat until the butter is melted, then set aside until lukewarm.

2   Put the flour and salt into a large mixing bowl and stir until thoroughly
combined. Make a well in the centre of the flour and sprinkle over
the yeast.

3   Pour the milk into the flour mixture, then add the egg and mix
thoroughly until it forms a smooth dough.

4   Tip the dough onto a lightly floured work surface and knead well for
10 minutes, until the dough is smooth and elastic, or use a dough
hook on a stand mixer and knead for 5-7 minutes. Place the dough
into an oiled bowl and leave to rise, covered with a damp tea towel,
for an hour, or until doubled in size.

5   Divide the dough into 8 equal pieces, then roll into oval buns.
Put on a baking tray lined with baking paper, then cover and leave
in a warm place to rise again for 30 minutes.

6   Preheat the oven to 180C/375F/gas mark 4. Brush the top of each bun
with milk, then bake for 25 minutes until golden and giving a hollow
sound when tapped on their bases. Allow to cool.

7   Brush each bun all over with melted butter, then roll in the caster sugar.
Split down the middle and spread generously with jam. Put the whipped
cream into a piping bag fitted with a star-shaped nozzle, then pipe into
the buns and serve.

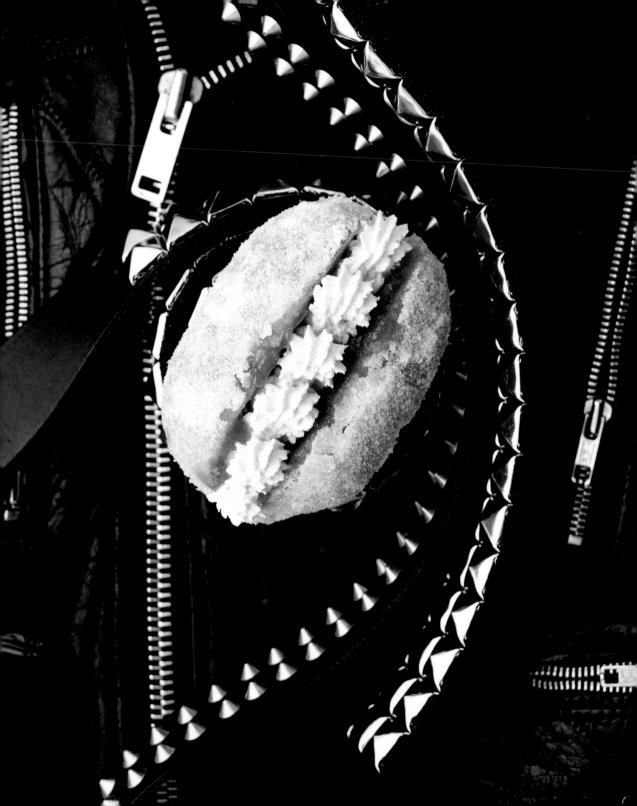

BAKE IN BLACK

Milk, white and dark chocolate lamingtons
with vanilla sponge and strawberry jam

Makes 12

For the sponge
200g plain flour
2 tsp baking powder
1 tsp salt
200g unsalted butter
175g caster sugar
1 tbsp vanilla bean paste
3 eggs
1-2 tbsp milk

To assemble
**½ jar good quality
strawberry jam**
**200g unsweetened
desiccated coconut**
**100g dark chocolate,
chopped**
**100g milk chocolate,
chopped**
**100g white chocolate,
chopped**

1   Preheat the oven to 180C/375F/gas mark 4. Line a 20cm x 20cm square tin with baking paper, then sift together the flour, baking powder and salt and set aside.

2   Using an electric whisk, beat the butter and sugar together until light and fluffy, then mix in the vanilla bean paste. Add the eggs one at a time, mixing until incorporated, then sift over the flour mixture and fold in. Add the milk to loosen, if necessary, then spoon into the tin and bake for 25 minutes, until golden and a skewer inserted into the middle comes out clean. Turn out onto a wire rack and let cool completely.

3   To assemble the lamingtons, slice the cake in half horizontally, then spread the bottom half generously with the strawberry jam and sandwich with the top half. Cut into 12 squares.

4   Tip the coconut into a shallow bowl, divide the lamingtons into three piles, then line a tray with baking paper. Melt one kind of chocolate at a time in a small glass bowl over a pan of simmering water.

5   Dip the first pile of lamingtons into the chocolate using two forks, rolling around to coat completely. Allow the chocolate to drip off, then roll in the coconut to cover. Repeat until all the lamingtons are coated in chocolate and coconut, then put the tray in the fridge until the chocolate has set.

CANNIBAL CORPSE

BAKED AT BIRTH

Rosehip-infused raspberry and
white chocolate blondies

Makes 12

150g raspberries
2 tbsp rosehip cordial
100g white chocolate,
chopped
100g unsalted butter, diced
2 eggs
300g caster sugar
200g self-raising flour

1 Preheat the oven to 160C/380F/gas mark 4, then butter and line
a 20cm x 20cm brownie tin.

2 Put the raspberries in a small bowl, then pour over the rosehip
cordial and set aside while you make the blondie batter.

3 In a glass bowl over, but not in, a pan of simmering water, melt
the chocolate and butter, stirring constantly to make sure it
doesn't separate.

4 Whisk the eggs with the caster sugar until pale and thick, then pour
in the chocolate mixture and stir until combined. Sift over the flour,
then fold through the raspberries and syrup.

5 Pour into the tin, then cook for 35 minutes, until just firm in the centre
with a harder crust around the edges. Allow to cool in the tin,
then remove and slice into pieces.

Rainbow

SINCE YOU'VE BAKED SCONES

Dried apple and fig scones with whipped butter, walnuts and honey

Makes 10-12

For the scones
230g plain flour, plus extra for dusting
2 tsp baking powder
Pinch of salt
½ tsp cinnamon
40g butter, diced and chilled
40g caster sugar
1 egg
100g dried apple slices, chopped
75g dried figs, roughly chopped
70ml milk

To glaze
2 tbsp milk
25g demerara sugar

To serve
100g unsalted butter, softened
1 tbsp icing sugar
1 tbsp milk
Honey, to serve
75g walnuts, toasted and roughly chopped (optional)

1   Preheat the oven to 220C/440F/gas mark 7. Line a baking tray with baking paper.

2   Sift the flour, baking powder, salt and cinnamon into a large mixing bowl, then, using your hands, rub the butter into the mix until it resembles fine breadcrumbs. Add the caster sugar and the egg, stir to combine, then add the dried apple pieces and figs. Gradually add the milk, a spoonful at a time, until the mix forms a dough.

3   On a lightly floured work surface, knead the scone dough gently, then roll out to around 2cm thick. Either stamp out 6cm circles using a biscuit cutter, or cut into squares or triangles. Place on the baking tray, then brush with milk and sprinkle with demerara sugar. Bake for around 12 minutes, until golden brown and risen. Allow to cool for 10 minutes on a wire rack.

4   While the scones are cooling, beat the butter, icing sugar and the milk together until light and fluffy. To serve, slice each scone in half, spread generously with whipped butter then drizzle with honey and scatter with walnuts.

LIMESLICE

Coconut shortbread and lime curd
paradise slices

Makes 12

For the lime curd
2 eggs and 2 egg yolks
Zest of 4 large limes
100ml lime juice
225g sugar
150g butter, cubed

For the shortbread
75g caster sugar
75g unsweetened
dessicated coconut
75g rice flour
Zest of 2 limes
150g butter
100g plain flour

For the coconut topping
100g plain flour
125g caster sugar
50g unsweetened
dessicated coconut
50g unsalted butter, diced

1   First, make the curd. Whisk the eggs and yolks with the lime zest, juice and sugar, then pour into a small saucepan. Cook over low heat, stirring constantly until the mixture thickens enough to coat the back of a wooden spoon, about 15 minutes. Remove from heat and whisk in the butter, one piece at a time, until smooth. Leave to cool; this will make more than you need, so store any leftovers in the fridge in an airtight container for up to two weeks.

2   Preheat the oven to 190C/380F/gas mark 5. To make the shortbread layer, mix the sugar, coconut, rice flour and lime zest with the butter, beating until light and fluffy, then add the flour, bit by bit, until it forms a dough, but be careful not to over-work. Press into a 20cm x 20cm tin, then chill in the fridge for 20 minutes. Prick with a fork, then bake for 15-20 minutes. Allow to cool completely in the tin.

3   Spread a layer of lime curd on top of the shortbread, then chill while you make the coconut crumble.

4   Mix the flour, sugar and coconut in a large bowl, then add the butter and rub with your fingers until the mix resembles rough breadcrumbs. Spread over a tray lined with baking paper, then bake at 190C/ 380F/gas mark 5 for 10-15 minutes, until golden and crunchy. Scatter the crumble topping over the shortbread, then chill for a couple of hours before slicing into bars.

Meat Loaf

BATTENBERG OUT OF HELL

Chocolate and raspberry Battenberg cake

Serves 8

175g unsalted butter, softened
175g caster sugar
175g self-raising flour
3 eggs
50g cocoa powder
4 tbsp Chambord liqueur
1 tube red food colouring gel
250g marzipan
150g raspberry jam

1   Heat the oven to 180C/375F/gas mark 4. Butter and line two 400g loaf tins, then set aside.

2   Mix the butter, sugar, flour and eggs. Divide in two and add 4 tbsp of the cocoa powder to one half and the red colouring and Chambord to the other. Spoon the chocolate mix into one tin and the raspberry into the other. Bake for 25 minutes, then cool in the tins for a short while and turn onto a wire rack to cool completely.

3   Knead the rest of cocoa powder into the marzipan until smooth and blended. Roll the marzipan to a rough rectangle – wide enough to cover the cakes when stacked. Lay one loaf on top of the other and trim both to the same size. Cut each cake into quarters lengthways, turn each on its side and cut in half lengthways again, so you end up with 8 long strips of each cake.

4   Lay a chocolate cake strip in the centre of the fondant and trim the fondant in a straight line at each end so it matches the length of the cake. Brush the cake all over with jam, lay a Chambord strip next to it and brush with jam, then another chocolate strip, and another Chambord strip. Push together tightly, brushing with more jam if you need it. Repeat until the cake is 3 'squares' high by 3 wide, then fold the fondant over the cake, brushing the overlapping fondant with jam to stick. Turn over so the seam is on the bottom, then carefully slice. There will be leftover cake slices, to allow for breakages and even slicing, but you can serve those with any remaining jam.

ALICE
IN
CHAINS

THEM BUNS

White chocolate, apricot and
orange swirl buns

Makes 8-10

For the buns
300ml milk
40g unsalted butter
500g strong white flour
1 tsp salt
7g sachet fast action yeast
1 egg, beaten

For the filling
**25g unsalted butter, melted
and cooled**
Zest of 1 orange
75g light brown sugar
**150g dried apricots,
finely chopped**
150g white chocolate chips

To finish
**100g white chocolate,
chopped**
1 heaped tbsp apricot jam

1   First, put the milk and butter in a small saucepan over a medium heat until the butter is melted, then set aside until lukewarm.

2   Put the flour and salt into a large mixing bowl and stir until thoroughly combined. Make a well in the centre of the flour and sprinkle over the yeast.

3   Pour the milk into the flour mixture, then add the egg and mix thoroughly until it forms a smooth dough.

4   Tip the dough onto a lightly floured work surface and knead well for 10 minutes, until the dough is smooth and elastic, or use a dough hook on a stand mixer and knead for 5-7 minutes. Place the dough into an oiled bowl and leave to rise, covered with a damp tea towel, for 1 hour or until doubled in size.

5   Tip the dough out onto a lightly floured work surface, then roll out into a rectangle of about 30 x 20cm. Brush all over with the butter, then sprinkle over the zest. Mix the sugar, apricots and white chocolate chips, then sprinkle evenly over the surface of the dough. Roll up quite tightly, pressing the ends together to stop too much filling from escaping, then cut the log into 8-10 rounds.

6   Lightly oil a large springform tin or a rectangular baking tray, then put the buns in the tin, leaving a 2cm space between. Cover them with a damp tea towel and let rise again in a warm place for 20-30 minutes. Preheat the oven to 180C/375F/gas mark 4.

7   Bake the buns for 35 minutes until golden and the white chocolate has leaked a little. To finish, melt the white chocolate in a glass bowl set over, but not in, a pan of simmering water. Allow to cool in the tin briefly before brushing with apricot jam and drizzling with the melted white chocolate.

I WAS MINT FOR LOVING YOU

White chocolate and mint brownies

Makes 12

For the brownies
100g plain flour
½ tsp salt
2 tbsp cocoa powder
120g dark chocolate, chopped
100g unsalted butter, diced
200g caster sugar
3 eggs
1 tsp vanilla extract

For the buttercream
150g caster sugar
2 tbsp plain flour
150ml whole milk
50ml double cream
150g unsalted butter, cubed
1-2 tbsp peppermint extract

For the glaze
200g white chocolate
50ml double cream

To decorate
Black, green and red icing pens (optional)

1   Heat the oven to 180C/375F/gas mark 4. Butter and line a 20cm x 30cm tin.

2   In a medium bowl, whisk the flour, salt and cocoa powder together and set aside.

3   Put the chocolate and butter in a glass bowl over, but not in, a pan of simmering water, then stir gently until melted. Take off the heat, then whisk in the sugar. Add the eggs and vanilla extract to the chocolate mixture, mixing until combined.

4   Add the dry ingredients to the bowl, then gently fold through, until completely mixed. Pour the batter into the tin – it should be quite a thin layer, around half the thickness of a normal brownie – then bake for about 15 minutes. The brownie should still be a little squidgy at this point. Allow to cool in the tin while you make the buttercream and glaze.

5   Mix the flour and sugar, then tip into a saucepan over a medium heat. Add the milk and cream then, whisking continuously, bring to almost boiling. Turn the heat down, then cook for around 5 minutes, whisking occasionally, until thickened – it should be custard-like.

6   Remove from the heat, then pour into a clean mixing bowl. Add the butter, then whisk until thoroughly combined. Stir in the peppermint extract to taste, then whisk again until light and fluffy. Chill in the fridge for 30 minutes if it is a little runny, then spread over the cooled brownie and chill for at least 1 hour.

7   To make the glaze, heat the cream in a small saucepan or microwave, then pour over the chopped white chocolate, stirring until smooth. Pour over the brownie, then return to the fridge for another hour to set. To serve, cut into squares, and decorate with KISS make up, if you like.

Status Quo

BLUEBERRY FOR YOU

Blueberry, lemon and soured cream
crumble muffins

Makes 12

For the muffins
60ml vegetable oil
1 egg
125ml soured cream
200g self-raising flour
175g caster sugar
1 tsp baking powder
Zest of 1 lemon
200g blueberries

For the crumble mixture
75g flour
Zest of 1 lemon
75g light brown sugar
75g oats
75g butter

1   Preheat the oven to 170C/350F/gas mark 4, then line a 12-hole muffin tray with paper cases.

2   To make the crumble topping, mix the flour, lemon zest, sugar and oats, then rub in the butter until the mix resembles breadcrumbs.

3   In large bowl, mix the oil, egg and soured cream, then sift together the dry ingredients and fold into the mixture until just combined. Stir through the blueberries, then spoon into the paper cases and top with the crumble mixture. Bake for 20-25 minutes, until golden brown.

THIN LIZZY

WHISKEY IN THE BAR

Californian raisin and whiskey brownies with an Irish cream liqueur glaze

Makes 12

For the brownies
150g Californian raisins
4 tbsp Irish whiskey
250g milk chocolate,
roughly chopped
200g butter
250g caster sugar
3 eggs
60g plain flour
60g cocoa powder
1 tsp baking powder

For the drizzle
50ml Irish cream liqueur
75g milk chocolate, chopped

1   Soak the raisins in the whiskey for at least 30 minutes, then heat the oven to 180C/375F/gas mark 4 and butter and line a 20cm x 20cm brownie tin.

2   Put the chocolate in a glass bowl over a pan of simmering water to melt gently. Beat the butter and sugar until pale and creamy, then while still beating, add the eggs, mix until combined, then, pour in the melted chocolate. Add the raisins and whiskey, then fold in the flour, cocoa and baking powder. Bake for 35-40 minutes, until just set in the middle. Allow to cool in the tin.

3   To make the drizzle, heat the cream liqueur in a pan until just bubbling, then pour over the chopped chocolate, stirring until smooth. Drizzle over the brownie, allow to harden for 10-15 minutes, then cut into bars.

RISE ABOVE

Vegan avocado, almond, lemon
and poppy seed loaves

Makes 10

1 large ripe hass avocado,
destoned and mashed
150g sweetened
dairy-free yoghurt
100ml vegetable oil
200g plain flour
1 tsp baking powder
150g ground almonds
A pinch of salt
75g caster sugar
Zest and juice of 1 lemon
3 tbsp poppy seeds,
plus extra to decorate

1   Preheat the oven to 180C/375F/gas mark 4. Mix the mashed
    avocado with the yoghurt and oil, then set aside.

2   In a large bowl, mix the flour, baking powder, ground almonds,
    salt, sugar, lemon zest and poppy seeds, then stir to combine.
    Add the avocado mix and lemon juice, then mix thoroughly.
    You might need a tbsp water to loosen – the batter should fall
    easily from a spoon. Pour into mini loaf cases and sprinkle with
    extra poppy seeds.

3   Bake in the oven for around 20-25 minutes, until a skewer inserted
    into one of the loaves comes out clean.

FAIRY CAKES WEAR BOOTLACES

Chocolate fairy cakes with blackberry and sloe buttercream

Makes 12

For the cakes
225g caster sugar
225g butter, melted
3 eggs
200g self-raising flour
30g cocoa powder
½ tsp salt

For the buttercream
150g unsalted butter
100g icing sugar
5 tbsp blackberry
and sloe jelly
2-3 drops of violet food
colouring
Berry-flavoured liquorice
laces or berry fruit leather,
to decorate

1 Heat the oven to 180C/375F/gas mark 4. Line a 12-hole muffin tin with paper cases. Beat the sugar and butter together with an electric whisk until light and fluffy, around 2-3 minutes, then add the eggs one at a time, beating until incorporated.

2 Sift the the flour, cocoa powder and salt together, then fold into the mixture, stirring until combined. Spoon into the muffin cases, then bake for 15-20 minutes, until a skewer inserted into a cake comes out clean. Cool on a wire rack.

3 To make the buttercream, beat the butter until light and fluffy, then gradually add the icing sugar. Add a few drops of colour and a spoon of jam until it becomes the desired shade. Put to one side.

4 To assemble the cakes, remove the paper cases from each cake, then stick the end of a lace to the bottom of one cake with buttercream and wrap around the cake until it is level with the top. Stick with more buttercream, or tuck into the lace below. Spread buttercream on top, leaving a slight dent in the centre, and add a teaspoon of jelly. Repeat with each cake.

BISCUITS AND COOKIES

CREAM GINGER BAKER CREAMS

DIO RONNIE PISTACH-DIO BISCOTTI

MASTODON CURL OF THE SWIRL

WHITE ZOMBIE THUNDER CHOCOLATE KISSES '65

BON JOVI I'M A COWBOY (COOKIE)

MARILYN MANSON SMELLS LIKE COOKIES

OBITUARY CHOPPED IN HALF

CHEAP TRICK I WANT CHEW TO WANT ME

CREAM

GINGER BAKER CREAMS

Ginger oat crackle biscuits with
a white chocolate buttercream filling

Makes 16

For the biscuits
160ml vegetable oil
200g golden caster sugar
1 egg
3½ tbsp black treacle
200g plain flour
200g jumbo rolled oats
2 tsp bicarbonate of soda
1 tsp ground cinnamon
3 tsp ground ginger
½ tsp ground cloves

For the filling
**100g white chocolate,
chopped**
**140g unsalted butter,
softened**
200g icing sugar

1   Preheat the oven to 180C/375F/gas mark 4 and line two baking
trays with baking paper.

2   Mix the oil and sugar, add the egg, and stir to combine. Then add
the black treacle, flour, oats, bicarbonate of soda and the spices.
Mix to a firm dough, then divide into 32 roughly equal pieces,
depending on how small or large you want the biscuits to be.
Roll into balls, then flatten into circles and bake for 10-12 minutes
until a dark golden colour, then cool on a wire rack.

3   While the biscuits are cooling, make the filling. Melt the white chocolate
over a pan of simmering water, then cool a little. Beat the butter with
an electric whisk until light and fluffy, then add the sugar bit by bit.
Slowly incorporate the white chocolate – if the mixture stiffens and
goes grainy, add a drop of boiling water and beat again.

4   Assemble the biscuits by spreading or piping the filling around the
outer edge of one, then sandwiching with another biscuit.

PISTACH-DIO BISCOTTI

Cranberry-studded Italian biscotti
with ground pistachios

Makes 14-16

**100g unsalted, shelled
pistachios
125g flour
1 tsp baking powder
Pinch of salt
75g caster sugar
1 egg, beaten
1 tbsp milk
50g dried cranberries,
roughly chopped**

1   Preheat the oven to 170C/340F/gas mark 3 and line a baking tray
    with baking paper. Measure out half the pistachios, then in a food
    processor, whizz the pistachios until finely ground. If doing by hand,
    finely chop the pistachios, then grind with a pestle and mortar until fine.
    Very roughly chop the other half.

2   In a large bowl, thoroughly mix the flour, baking powder, salt, sugar
    and ground pistachios. Mix in the egg and milk, then add the chopped
    pistachios and cranberries. Mix to a dough, then shape into a log,
    around 5-6cm in width.

3   Put onto the baking tray and bake for around 30 minutes until golden.
    Allow to cool on the tray for 10 minutes or so, then transfer to a wire
    rack to cool completely.

4   Turn the oven down to 150C/320F/gas mark 2. Line another baking
    tray with baking paper, then cut the log into diagonal slices, around
    1cm wide. Put on the baking tray, then return to the oven for another
    30 minutes, until crisp. Cool on a wire rack, then store in an airtight
    container – they should keep for a good week.

MASTODON

CURL OF THE SWIRL

Chocolate and malted milk
swirl cookies

Makes 16

250g butter
200g sugar
A pinch of salt
1 tsp vanilla extract
200g flour
100g malted milk powder
75g cocoa powder
1-2 tbsp milk, if needed

1   Preheat the oven to 190C/380F/gas mark 5. Line two baking trays with baking paper.

2   In a large bowl, beat the butter and sugar with an electric whisk until light and fluffy, then add the salt and vanilla and beat again to incorporate. Beat in the flour until just incorporated, then divide the mix between two bowls.

3   Stir the cocoa through one mix and the malted milk powder through another, loosening with milk, if needed. Put the chocolate mix back in with the malted mix, then gently swirl together, until marbled.

4   Using an ice cream scoop, spoon out balls of dough on to the prepared baking trays, leaving a 2cm gap between them, then bake for 12-15 minutes, until firm and lightly golden on the malted dough. Allow to cool on a wire rack.

WHITE ZOMBIE

THUNDER CHOCOLATE KISSES '65

Chocolate kisses with marshmallow centres

Makes 8

For the biscuits
**150g self-raising flour
2 tbsp cocoa powder
100g unsalted butter, diced
30g caster sugar
1 egg, beaten
1-2 tbsp milk**

For the filling
**1 jar marshmallow spread
Lime, violet and yellow
food colouring**

1 Heat the oven to 160C/350F/gas mark 3. Line two baking trays with baking paper.

2 Sift the flour and cocoa powder into a mixing bowl, then add the diced butter. Rub it into the flour until the mix resembles fine breadcrumbs, then mix in the sugar. Add the egg and a little of the milk, until it forms a slightly sticky dough. Roll into around 16 balls, then put on the baking sheets. Flatten each with the tines of a fork, then bake for around 12 minutes. Let cool on the trays for 5 minutes and transfer to a wire rack to cool completely.

3 To make the filling, divide the spread between 3 bowls, then add the different colourings to each until you have the desired shades. Sandwich the cooled cookies together with the marshmallow colours, then eat immediately, before the filling runs.

Illustration by Rob Zombie

I'M A COWBOY (COOKIE)

Chocolate, coconut, peanut butter and pecan cowboy cookies

Makes 24

275g plain flour
150g jumbo rolled oats
75g desiccated coconut
1½ tsp bicarbonate of soda
1½ tsp baking powder
1½ tsp flaked sea salt
175g unsalted butter
175g light brown sugar
150g caster sugar
2 eggs
2 tsp vanilla extract
150g pecans, toasted and roughly chopped
300g plain chocolate, chopped
200g peanut butter chips

1   Preheat the oven to 180C/375F/gas mark 4 and line two baking trays with baking paper.

2   Mix together the flour, oats, coconut, bicarbonate of soda, baking powder and salt. Beat the butter and sugars together with an electric whisk until light and fluffy. Add eggs, one at a time, mixing well after each addition, then mix in the vanilla. Add the dry ingredients and stir to combine. At this stage you can keep the dough in the fridge for up to 3 days, until ready to bake.

3   Put heaped tablespoons of dough about 3cm apart on the trays, then bake for 14-16 minutes (if you want a really chewy cookie, bake for no longer than 14 minutes).

MARILYN
MANSON

SMELLS LIKE COOKIES

Blueberry and soured cream swirl
sandwich biscuits

Makes 8-10

For the biscuits
**250g unsalted butter,
softened
75g icing sugar
200g self-raising flour
50g cornflour
1 tsp vanilla extract
½-1 tsp violet or pink gel
food colouring**

For the filling
**2 tbsp unsalted, pale butter
2 tbsp vegetable shortening
150g icing sugar,
100ml soured cream
Blueberry jam, to serve**

1 Preheat the oven to 190C/375F/gas mark 4 and line a baking tray with baking paper. Using a 6cm biscuit cutter, trace about 16 circles (or more smaller, bite-sized circles, if you like) onto the baking paper, leaving around 1cm between each. Turn the baking paper onto the other side, so the trace comes through but the biscuit dough won't touch the pencil lead.

2 In a large bowl, beat the butter and sugar with an electric whisk until light, fluffy and quite soft, then add the vanilla and beat again to incorporate. Sift the flours together then add gradually until the dough comes together. Remove ⅓ of the dough from the bowl and mix in the food colouring until the colour is uniform.

3 Working quickly, fit a large, star-shaped nozzle to a piping bag. Then invert the piping bag, and press the coloured dough around the sides of the bag. Push the plain dough into the middle of the piping bag, then pipe swirls within each circle onto the baking tray. Bake for 15 minutes, or until lightly golden, then cool on a wire rack.

4 To make the soured cream filling, cream the butter and vegetable shortening until light and fluffy, then gradually add the icing sugar and soured cream, alternating between the two to make sure the buttercream is thick enough.

5 To assemble, spread a layer of filling on the bottom of one biscuit, spread the jam on another then sandwich together. Repeat until all the biscuits are used.

OBITUARY

CHOPPED IN HALF

Date, honey and sesame
shortbread rolls

Makes 20

For the biscuit dough
100g plain flour
100g spelt flour
A pinch of salt
Zest of 1 lemon
60g caster sugar
**100g unsalted butter, diced
and chilled**
50ml water

For the filling
125g dates, roughly chopped
175ml water
1 tbsp brandy
2 tbsp honey
2 tbsp sesame seeds

1   To make the filling, put the dates, water, brandy and honey in a small saucepan, then cook over a low heat for around 20 minutes, until the dates have softened and broken down a little, and most of the water has evaporated. Take off the heat, stir through the sesame seeds then allow to cool.

2   Preheat the oven to 180C/375F/gas mark 4, then line 2 baking trays with baking paper. Sift the flours and salt into a large bowl, then mix in the lemon zest and sugar. Add the butter, then rub into the mix with your hands until it resembles fine breadcrumbs. Add the water a little at a time, until the mix forms a dough. Wrap in clingfilm then chill for 30 minutes.

3   Once chilled, roll the dough out on a floured work surface to a rectangle, around 1cm thick and 10cm in width. Spread the cooled date filling over the dough, then roll up as tightly as possible. Slice into 2cm rounds, then cook for 15-20 minutes, until golden. Cool on a wire rack.

Cheap Trick

I WANT CHEW TO WANT ME

Chocolate, coffee and hazelnut shortbread

Makes 12

150g unsalted butter, softened
75g caster sugar
1 tsp vanilla extract
½ tsp salt
120g plain flour
100g ground hazelnuts
2 tbsp cocoa powder
1½ tsp instant coffee, finely ground
1 tube black gel food colouring
1 egg, beaten

1   Beat the butter and sugar until light and creamy, then add the vanilla extract and salt. Gradually add the flour and ground hazelnuts and work into a dough.

2   Mix the cocoa powder with the instant coffee. Divide the dough in half, then sprinkle the cocoa and coffee mix over one half, then knead until incorporated. Add a few drops of black gel colouring to this half of the dough, then knead until the colour is mixed in and smooth. Add a tiny splash of milk if it's a little stiffer than the vanilla dough. Chill in the fridge for 30 minutes.

3   Place each half of dough between two long pieces of clingfilm, then roll each piece out into two 18 cm squares, about 1½ cm thick. Using a sharp knife and a ruler, slice each square into nine strips.

4   Lay a large piece of clingfilm on the work surface. Put three strips of dough on the clingfilm side by side, alternating vanilla and chocolate/coffee strips. Brush the tops of the strips with a little beaten egg, then gently press the strips together. Repeat, forming five more layers. You should end up with a chequerboard of three squares by five squares. Wrap the dough tightly in clingfilm then chill for 1 hour, or put in the freezer to bake another time.

5   Preheat oven to 180C/375F/gas mark 4. Line a baking tray with baking paper. Slice the dough into ½-cm-thick slices then carefully place on the baking tray and cook for 10-12 minutes, until the vanilla shortbread is a light golden colour. Transfer to a wire rack to cool completely.

DOUGHNUTS

METALLICA BAKE 'EM ALL

NOFX WHITE CHOC, TWO SEEDS AND A VANILLA BEAN

PANTERA FAR BEYOND RISEN

HOLE VIOLET DOUGHNUT HOLES

BAD BRAINS BAKED IN D.C.

JIMI HENDRIX MAPLE GLAZE

SKID ROW YEAST GONE WILD

LED ZEPPELIN GLAZED AND INFUSED

METALLICA

BAKE 'EM ALL
Baked doughnuts with raspberry
and redcurrant jelly

Makes 12

For the doughnuts
500g plain flour
7g sachet fast action yeast
40g caster sugar
1 tsp salt
300ml milk
50g butter
1 egg, beaten

For the jelly
250g raspberries
250g redcurrants,
stalks removed
350g jam sugar

To finish
50g butter, melted
100g caster sugar

1 To make the jelly, put the fruit in a saucepan and simmer over
a medium heat for 10 minutes, until the fruit has broken down.
Take off the heat then pour into a muslin. Squeeze the liquid
through, then discard the remains.

2 Put the fruit liquid back into the saucepan, add the sugar, and
bring to the boil, stirring constantly. Once thickened, put in an
airtight container and allow to cool completely.

3 To make the doughnuts, mix the flour, yeast, sugar and salt in
a large bowl, then set aside.

4 Pour the milk into a saucepan, and warm gently. Add the butter,
stirring until melted, then take off the heat and cool to lukewarm.
Stir in the egg, then tip into the dry ingredients and mix to a dough.
Knead on a floured work surface for around 10 minutes, or until
elastic and smooth, or knead in a stand mixer with a dough hook for
5-7 minutes. Put into a clean, oiled bowl, cover with a cloth or clingfilm
then let rise in a warm place for 1 hour, until doubled in size.

5 Take the dough out of the bowl then knock back a little. Roll out on
a floured work surface, to about 2cm thick, then using a 6cm biscuit
cutter, cut out 12 doughnuts. Put onto a baking tray lined with baking
paper, cover with clingfilm then leave to rise again for 30 minutes.

6 Preheat the oven to 180C/375F/gas mark 4, then bake the
doughnuts for around 15 minutes, until golden. Transfer to a wire
rack to cool a little, then put the melted butter in one bowl, and the
sugar in another. Working quickly, roll the doughnuts in the butter,
then the sugar, and allow to cool on a wire rack.

7 To fill the doughnuts, make a small incision in the side of each.
Spoon the jelly into a piping bag. Squeeze the jelly to the end,
then snip off the end of the bag and fill each doughnut with jelly.

WHITE CHOC, TWO SEEDS AND A VANILLA BEAN

Vanilla and poppy seed doughnuts with white chocolate and cardamom glaze

Makes 12

For the doughnuts
250g plain flour
150g caster sugar
1 tsp baking powder
1 tsp bicarbonate of soda
2 tbsp poppy seeds
1 tsp salt
2 tbsp vanilla bean paste
2 eggs, beaten
200ml milk
30g butter, melted

For the glaze
150g white chocolate
2 tsp ground cardamom
50-75ml double cream
Natural pink food colouring

1 Heat the oven to 180C/375F/gas mark 4. Lightly butter 2 six-hole doughnut pans, or if you don't have a doughnut pan, line a 12-hole muffin tin with paper cases.

2 Mix the flour, sugar, baking powder, bicarbonate of soda, poppy seeds and salt into a large bowl. Mix the vanilla paste, eggs, milk and butter together, then tip into the dry ingredients, mixing well, until incorporated.

3 Carefully spoon the mix into the doughnut pan, filling each hole about ⅔ full. Cook for 10-12 minutes until the doughnuts are golden brown. Leave for 5 minutes to cool in the tin, then turn out onto a wire rack to cool completely.

4 To make the glaze, put the white chocolate in a glass bowl over, but not in, a pan of simmering water to melt, then stir in the ground cardamom. Cool a little, then add the double cream, bit by bit, until it has a thick pouring consistency. Add a few drops of food colouring until you've got the colour you like, then drizzle over the doughnuts.

FAR BEYOND RISEN

Almond, pecan and cinnamon
bear claw doughnuts

Makes 6

For the doughnuts
350g plain flour
7g sachet fast action yeast
40g caster sugar
1 tsp salt
75ml lukewarm milk
2 eggs
1 tsp vanilla extract
60g unsalted butter, softened

For the filling
100g almond butter
70g pecans, chopped
50g caster sugar
½ tsp cinnamon

To finish
100g caster sugar
1 tsp cinnamon
A large handful of whole pecans, for the claws
50g butter, melted

1   Put the flour, yeast, sugar and salt in a large mixing bowl, then stir to combine. Add the milk, eggs and vanilla, then mix to a rough dough. Knead for 10 minutes by hand, or 5-7 minutes in a stand mixer, using a dough hook, until it is smooth and elastic and no longer sticks to your hands.

2   Add the softened butter, then knead into the dough until completely incorporated. It will be a little messy, but the butter will eventually mix in. Put in a clean, oiled bowl, cover with clingfilm, and leave to rise in a warm place for 1 hour, or until doubled in size.

3   Once doubled, punch the dough down a bit, knead briefly, then cover again and chill for 4-12 hours (you can make the dough in the evening, then chill overnight, ready for breakfast in the morning).

4   Once chilled, cut the dough into three pieces, then roll each into a large rectangle. Gently heat the almond butter in a small saucepan, until slightly looser, then spread evenly over the dough and scatter with the pecans, cinnamon and sugar. Fold lengthways by thirds, pinching the edges together to hold the filling. Cut each third in half, then put seam-side down on a baking sheet. Make three slashes in each doughnut to resemble claws. Cover and let rise for 45 minutes.

5   Preheat the oven to 180C/375F/gas mark 4. Mix the sugar with the cinnamon, then set aside. Push a whole pecan into each 'finger' (make a small incision with a knife if you need to), then bake for 25 minutes, until golden. Once cooled a little, brush with melted butter, then roll in the cinnamon sugar.

VIOLET DOUGHNUT HOLES

Vanilla doughnut holes with white chocolate and violet dip

Serves 8

For the doughnuts
500g plain flour
30g sugar
7g sachet fast action yeast
1 tsp salt
250ml whole milk
2 tbsp unsalted butter
1 egg
1 tbsp vanilla bean paste
1 litre vegetable oil,
for frying
Vanilla sugar, for rolling

For the dip
200g good-quality white
chocolate, roughly chopped
150ml double cream
3 tbsp violet syrup or
blueberry jam

1 Mix the flour, sugar, yeast and salt in a large bowl, then set aside.

2 Gently warm the milk in a small saucepan, then add the butter and stir until melted. Remove from the heat, then, when cooled to lukewarm, beat in the egg and vanilla bean paste.

3 Tip the milk mixture into the flour, then mix to a sticky dough. Knead on a floured work surface for 10 minutes, until smooth and elastic, or knead in a stand mixer with a dough hook for 5-7 minutes. Place into an oiled bowl and set aside in a warm place for about an hour, until doubled in size.

4 Knead the dough for a minute or two, until knocked back, then roll out on a floured surface and, using a small biscuit cutter, stamp into 2cm diameter circles. Place on a baking tray lined with baking paper, loosely cover with clingfilm and leave to rise again, in a warm place, for 30 minutes.

5 Tip the vanilla sugar onto a plate, then spread out evenly. Heat the oil in a saucepan to 180C, or until a breadcrumb sizzles and turns crisp and golden within 30 seconds. Fry the doughnut holes in batches of 4-5, around 2-3 minutes, until crisp and golden, then drain on kitchen paper and, while still hot, roll in the vanilla sugar. Keep them warm while you make the dip.

6 Put the chocolate into a small bowl, then pour the double cream into a saucepan, heat until just boiling then pour over the white chocolate and let stand for a minute. Stir until melted and smooth.

7 Put the white chocolate into a small serving bowl, swirl through the violet syrup, then serve with the warm doughnut holes.

BAKED IN D.C.

Ginger, cinnamon and all-spice
pull-apart doughnuts

Serves 10

For the doughnuts
250ml milk
75g butter
500g plain flour
7g sachet fast action yeast
60g caster sugar
1 tsp salt
1 egg

For the coating
120g unsalted butter, melted
1 tsp ground ginger
1 tsp cinnamon
2 tsp allspice
½ tsp ground cloves
150g dark brown sugar

1 In a small pan, warm the milk to just above room temperature with the butter, until melted, then remove from the heat. Cool to lukewarm.

2 Mix the flour, yeast, sugar and salt. Whisk the egg into the milk mixture, then stir into the flour and mix until it forms a dough. Knead for about 10 minutes, until the dough is smooth and elastic, or knead in a stand mixer with a dough hook for 5-7 minutes. Put in a clean, oiled bowl, cover with clingfilm and leave in a warm place to rise until doubled in size, about an hour.

3 Line a baking tray with baking paper. Cut the dough in half, then cut each half into about 25 pieces. Roll each into a small sphere, about the size of a ping pong ball, and put on the baking paper. Cover these as you go with a tea towel or clingfilm to stop them drying out.

4 To make the coating, put the melted butter in a small bowl, and mix the spices and sugar in another. Take a ball and dip it in the butter, then coat in the spiced sugar and put in the bundt tin. Repeat with the other balls until they are evenly spread across the whole tin but tightly packed. At this point, you can chill in the fridge for a few hours or overnight, or continue to cook.

5 Cover the bundt tin in clingfilm and leave to rise again for an hour, whether chilled or not.

6 Heat the oven to 180C/375F/gas mark 4, then bake for 30 minutes, until the sugar is bubbling at the sides and golden.

MAPLE GLAZE

French cruller doughnuts
with a maple glaze

Makes 8

For the crullers
250ml water
80g butter
200g flour
4 eggs, beaten
1 litre vegetable oil,
for frying

For the glaze
200g icing sugar
2-3 tbsp maple syrup
2-3 tbsp water

1   In a medium saucepan, mix the water and butter then put over a medium heat and bring to the boil. Once boiling, stir in the flour, beating continuously as you go to avoid any lumps.

2   Once the flour is incorporated, remove from the heat and beat in the eggs, one at a time, until the mixture is smooth and shiny.

3   Put the dough into a piping bag fitted with a very large star-shaped nozzle, then pipe small circles in a clockwise motion, around 5cm in diameter, onto baking paper. Pipe another identical circle anticlockwise on top of each, then put in the freezer for 15 minutes to harden while you heat the oil.

4   To cook the crullers, heat the oil in a saucepan to 180C, or until a breadcrumb sizzles and turns crisp and golden within 30 seconds. Fry the crullers in batches of 3-4, around 2-3 minutes, until crisp and golden, then drain on kitchen paper.

5   To make the glaze, whisk the icing sugar, maple syrup and water together, then submerge each cruller fully in the mix to evenly glaze and put on a wire rack or plate. Allow to harden a little, then eat.

YEAST GONE WILD

Sourdough doughnuts with peaches and cream filling

Makes 12

For the doughnuts
**200g strong white flour,
plus extra for rolling
1 tsp salt
60g caster sugar
½ tsp bicarbonate of soda
250g sourdough starter
240ml milk
2 eggs, beaten
750ml vegetable oil,
for frying
100g vanilla sugar or caster
sugar, for rolling**

For the filling
**200ml whole milk
1 vanilla pod, split
lengthways, seeds
scraped out
2 egg yolks
40g caster sugar
4-5 tbsp peach compote
or jam**

1 First, make the filling. Put the milk in a small saucepan with the vanilla pod and seeds, bring to the boil then take off the heat and set to one side, to infuse, for 15 minutes.

2 Lightly whisk the eggs and sugar together, then pour the slightly cooled milk mixture (with the vanilla pod fished out, if using) into the mix. Whisk together, then pour back into a clean saucepan and cook over a low heat, stirring frequently, until thickened, around 5 minutes. Once cooked, pour into a bowl and press clingfilm over the top of the custard to stop a skin forming. Once cool, stir the peach compote through the custard to create a rippled effect, as opposed to fully combining, cover again with clingfilm and set aside.

3 To make the doughnuts, mix the flour, salt, sugar and bicarbonate of soda together, then mix with the sourdough starter and milk. Beat in the eggs, then mix to a smooth dough and knead for a couple of minutes. Put in a clean, oiled bowl and allow to rise in a warm place for an hour, or until the mix has doubled.

4 Once risen, punch the dough back down a little on a floured surface, roll out to around 3cm thickness, then stamp into 8-10cm rounds with a biscuit cutter.

5 To cook the doughnuts, heat the oil in a saucepan until 180C, or a breadcrumb sizzles and turns crisp and golden within 30 seconds. Fry the doughnut in batches, around 4-5 minutes, until crisp and golden, then drain on kitchen paper and roll in the sugar while still hot.

6 Poke a hole in the side of each doughnut with a skewer, wiggling around a little to create more space for the filling. Put the filling in a piping bag with a smallish, plain nozzle, then pipe the cream into the centre of each doughnut, until filled.

Led Zeppelin

GLAZED AND INFUSED

Lavender-infused ring doughnuts
with milk chocolate glaze

Makes 12

For the doughnuts
500g plain flour
1 tsp salt
40g caster sugar
7g sachet dried yeast
300ml whole milk
2 sprigs of lavender
40g unsalted butter
1 egg
1 litre vegetable oil,
for frying

For the glaze
100g milk chocolate,
chopped

1   In a large bowl, mix the flour, salt and caster sugar, then make
a well in the centre and scatter in the yeast.

2   Put the milk in a small saucepan with the lavender, then gently heat,
adding the butter after a couple of minutes. Once the butter has melted,
remove from the heat, fish out the lavender and allow the mixture to
cool to lukewarm before pouring into the flour mixture with the egg.
Mix to a sticky dough, then knead on a floured work surface for 10
minutes, until smooth and elastic, or knead in a stand mixer with a
dough hook for 5-7 minutes. Place into an oiled bowl and set aside
in a warm place for about an hour, until doubled in size.

3   Knock the dough back a little, then roll out on a floured surface and,
using a biscuit cutter, stamp into 6cm diameter circles, then poke a 1cm
diameter hole in the middle of each. Place on a baking tray lined with
baking paper, loosely cover with clingfilm and leave to rise again in
a warm place for 25-30 minutes.

4   Heat the oil in a saucepan until 180C, or a breadcrumb sizzles,
and turns crisp and golden within 30 seconds. Fry the doughnuts
in batches, around 3-4 minutes, until crisp and golden, then drain
on kitchen paper while you make the glaze.

5   Put the chocolate in a small glass bowl, then put over, but not in,
a pan of simmering water and gently melt.

6   Dunk the top of each doughnut in the glaze, twisting to ensure
an even coverage, then put on a plate and allow to set a little
before eating.

PIES

SMASHING PUMPKINS PIAMESE DREAM

DEF LEPPARD POUR SOME SUGAR ON ME

VAN HALEN HOT FOR TEACHER HAND PIES

MOTÖRHEAD LEMMY'S MERINGUE PIE

GREEN DAY BASKET CASE

DEFTONES CHANGE (IN THE HOUSE OF PIES)

FAITH NO MORE FAITH NO S'MORE

DARKTHRONE A BLAZE IN THE NORTHERN PIE

PIAMESE DREAM

Spiced pumpkin and stem
ginger pie

Serves 8

For the filling
½ pumpkin, seeded
2 eggs, beaten
397g tin condensed milk
1 tsp cinnamon
½ tsp ground cloves
½ tsp ground allspice
2 tbsp stem ginger syrup

For the pastry
225g plain flour
A pinch of salt
100g butter, diced
3-4 tbsp cold water

1 To make the pastry, mix the flour and salt, then rub the butter into the flour with your hands until it resembles fine breadcrumbs. Gradually add the water until it can be worked into a smooth dough, then use to line a 23cm round or rectangular tart tin. Chill while you make the filling.

2 Preheat the oven to 200C/400F/gas mark 6, then put slices of pumpkin in a roasting tin and cook for around 1 hour, until the flesh is tender. Scoop the flesh from the skin, then blend to a smooth puree and allow to cool.

3 Once the pumpkin puree has cooled, weigh out 500g, then mix with the eggs, condensed milk, spices and ginger syrup, and pour into the tart tin.

4 Reduce the heat of the oven to 180C/375F/gas mark 4, then cook for around 35-45 minutes, until just set in the centre. Allow to cool, then serve.

POUR SOME SUGAR ON ME

Sour black cherry and cinnamon pie

Serves 6

For the pastry
150g plain flour
A pinch of salt
50g icing sugar
150g unsalted butter, diced and chilled
1 egg yolk
1-2 tbsp water
2-3 tbsp milk
30g Demerara sugar

For the filling
450g fresh or frozen cherries, stones removed and halved
75g dried sour cherries
1 tbsp flour
1 tsp cinnamon

To serve
1 tub vanilla ice cream

1   To make the pastry, put the flour, salt and sugar in a bowl, add the butter and rub in until it resembles fine breadcrumbs. Add the yolk and a couple of tsps of water, mix to a dough, wrap in clingfilm then chill in the fridge for 30 minutes.

2   Preheat the oven to 180C/375F/gas mark 4. Break off ⅔ of the pastry, then roll out to around 1cm thick and use to line an 18cm tart tin.

3   In a large bowl, mix the fresh and dried cherries, then sprinkle over the flour and cinnamon and toss until thoroughly combined. Spoon into the pie tin, then roll out the remaining ⅓ of pastry to the same thickness, and wide enough to cover the pie tin.

4   Brush the edges of the pastry in the tin with a little milk, then cover with the pastry lid. Crimp the edges of the pastry to seal, snip a hole in the centre to let steam escape, then brush with more milk and scatter the sugar over the top. Bake for 30 minutes, or until the pastry is crisp and golden. Serve with vanilla ice cream.

HOT FOR TEACHER HAND PIES

Apple, rosemary and pecan hand pies

Makes 6

2 tbsp salted butter
2 Pink Lady or
Golden Delicious apples,
peeled, cored and diced
1 Granny Smith apple,
peeled, cored and diced
2 tsp finely chopped
fresh rosemary
2 tbsp dark brown sugar
60ml maple syrup
1 tbsp flour
Juice of half a lemon
100g pecans, finely chopped
375g shortcrust pastry
1 egg, beaten

1 Preheat the oven to 200C/400F/gas mark 6. Heat the butter in a large, heavy-based frying pan. Once foaming, add the apples, rosemary, sugar and maple syrup and cook down for around 5-10 minutes, until the apples are soft but still just holding their shape.

2 Add the flour, stir to coat the apples then cook for another 2 minutes, until the juice coming from the apples has thickened. Add a squeeze of lemon, stir through the pecans then set aside to cool.

3 Roll out the shortcrust pastry on a floured surface to a 25cm x 25cm rectangle, then cut into 6 pieces. Brush the egg around the edges of the first piece of pastry, then put a couple of heaped spoonfuls of the apple mixture on the left half of the rectangle. Fold over the right half to form a smaller rectangle, then press together the edges of the pastry with the tines of a fork, and snip tiny holes in the middle of each to allow steam to escape. Repeat with the rest of the pastry and the apple mixture.

4 Transfer the pies to a baking tray lined with baking paper, brush the tops with the remaining egg wash then bake in the oven for 25 minutes, until golden.

LEMMY'S MERINGUE PIE

Cider and black forest fruit
meringue pie

Serves 6

For the pastry
125g plain flour
A pinch of salt
25g icing sugar
75g very cold unsalted
butter, cubed
1 egg yolk

For the filling
350g frozen blackcurrants
or forest fruits
250ml medium-sweet cider
2-3 tbsp icing sugar, to taste
60g cornflour

For the meringue
6 egg whites
175g caster sugar

1 To make the pastry, put the flour, salt and sugar in a bowl, add the butter and rub in until it resembles fine breadcrumbs. Add the egg yolk and a couple of tsps of water, mix to a dough, wrap in clingfilm then chill in the fridge for 30 minutes.

2 Use the pastry to line a 20cm tart tin, making sure there are no holes and the pastry is level with the top of the tin, then chill again for an hour. Preheat the oven to 170C/350F/gas mark 3, then line the pastry with baking paper and baking beans. Bake for 15 minutes, remove the paper and beans then bake for a further 10 minutes.

3 Put the forest fruits in a saucepan with the cider and sugar then simmer over a medium heat for about 30 minutes, until the fruit has broken down a little. Remove from the heat, strain the juice back into the pan and set the fruit pieces aside, then return to the heat and whisk in the cornflour until you have a very thick sauce. Pour the sauce over the reserved fruit and allow to cool.

4 To make the meringue, beat the egg whites to soft peaks, then add the sugar a little at a time, beating for at least 2 minutes in between each addition. The meringue should be thick and glossy.

5 Put the filling in the pastry case, top with the meringue then return to the oven at 180C/375F/gas mark 4 for 15 minutes, until the meringue is scorched to your liking.

BASKET CASE

Apricot and elderflower lattice pie
with almond pastry

Serves 6-8

For the pastry
240g flour
1 tsp salt
150g icing sugar
100g ground almonds
200g butter, diced and chilled
1 egg yolk
3-5 tbsp water
2 tbsp milk, for glazing

For the filling
25g butter
500g apricots, destoned and quartered
4 tbsp elderflower cordial
1 tbsp caster sugar

To serve
300ml double cream
1 tbsp elderflower cordial

1 To make the pastry, mix the flour, salt, icing sugar and ground almonds in a large bowl, then add the butter and rub it into the mix until it resembles fine breadcrumbs. Add the egg yolk and the water and mix to a dough. Wrap in clingfilm then chill in the fridge while you make the filling.

2 In a large frying pan, gently melt the butter until foaming, then add the apricots. Cook for 5 minutes or so, then add the elderflower cordial and sugar. Cook for another 5 minutes, until the apricots have softened and broken down a little. Take off the heat, check to taste (adding more cordial if it needs it).

3 Preheat the oven to 190C/380F/gas mark 5. Break off ⅔ of the pastry, then roll out to a ½ cm thick disc, wide enough to line an 18cm fluted tart dish or tin. Roll out the remaining pastry to the same thickness, then cut into 14, 2cm wide strips.

4 Spoon the filling into the pie and smooth the top. Put a large piece of baking paper on the work surface, then weave strips of pastry across it in a lattice pattern. Using a cake slice, slide the pastry onto the top of the tart, brush with milk, then bake for 30 minutes, until golden.

5 Whip the double cream with the elderflower cordial, cut the pie into wedges and serve with a dollop of cream.

CHANGE (IN THE HOUSE OF PIES)

Chai-spiced pecan pie with maple syrup

Serves 8

375g block shortcrust pastry
2 tbsp plain flour
3 tbsp salted butter, softened
to room temperature
100g sugar
200g maple syrup
100g golden syrup
3 eggs, beaten
1 tsp ground cardamom
½ tsp ground ginger
½ tsp ground cinnamon
¼ tsp ground cloves
350g pecans

1 Preheat the oven to 180C/375F/gas mark 4. Roll the pastry out onto a lightly floured surface to a 1cm thickness, then use to line a 20cm loose-bottomed tart tin. Line with baking paper and baking beans, then cook for 15 minutes. Remove the baking paper and baking beans, then return to the oven for 10 minutes, then allow to cool while you make the filling.

2 Beat the butter and sugar together until light and fluffy, then add both the syrups, eggs and the spices, mixing until smooth. Stir through ¾ of the pecans, spoon into the tin, then decorate the top of the pie with the rest of the pecans.

3 Bake for 40-45 minutes, until firm and golden all over. Allow to cool completely, then cut into wedges to serve.

darkthrone

A BLAZE IN THE NORTHERN PIE

Rhubarb, cardamom and custard pie

Serves 4

375g block sweet shortcrust pastry
Flour, for rolling
100ml cream
75ml whole milk
5 cardamom pods, lightly crushed
75g caster sugar
2 eggs
8-10 stalks of pink rhubarb, peeled into thin strips, lengthways

1   Preheat the oven to 180C/375F/gas mark 4. Roll out the pastry to around ½cm thickness, then use it to line an 18cm tart tin. Chill for 10 minutes, then line with baking paper, add baking beans or dried beans to weigh the pastry down, then cook for 15 minutes. Remove the baking paper and beans from the pastry, then bake for another 10 minutes, until pale and golden, and set aside.

2   Put the cream, milk and cardamom in a saucepan, bring to the boil then remove from the heat, fish out the cardamom pods and allow to cool a little.

3   Beat the sugar and eggs with an electric whisk until light and fluffy, then pour over the cream mixture, whisking to combine.

4   Pack the strips of rhubarb into the tin from the centre out, creating tightly fitting circles, working your way to the outside, until all the rhubarb is tightly packed and used up. Pour the custard mixture over the rhubarb, being careful not to overfill, then bake for 30-40 minutes, until the tart is firm and the rhubarb is tender. Cool a little, or chill until cold, if you'd prefer, then serve.

FAITH NO S'MORE

Chocolate cream pie with a marshmallow topping

Serves 8

375g block sweet
shortcrust pastry
Flour, for rolling
200g dark chocolate,
chopped
100g milk chocolate,
chopped
300ml double cream
2 eggs
A pinch of salt
A small bag
of marshmallows

1 Preheat the oven to 180C/375F/gas mark 4. Roll the pastry out to ½ cm thickness, then use to line a 23cm pastry case. Chill while you make the filling.

2 Put the 2 chopped chocolates in separate bowls, then bring the cream to the boil. Once boiling, pour into a measuring jug, then add 200ml cream to the dark chocolate, and 100ml to the milk chocolate. Let stand for a minute or so, then stir each chocolate, separately, to combine.

3 Whisk the eggs into the dark chocolate, then pour into the pastry case. Add blobs of the milk chocolate mixture to the tin, then swirl gently to give a marbled effect. Bake for 25-30 minutes, until the pastry is golden and the mixture is almost firm. Allow to cool a little, then chill in the fridge until set.

4 To make the topping, heat the grill to high, then top the pie with marshmallows, so it covers the surface evenly. Put small pieces of foil around the pastry edges to prevent them from burning, then put the pie under the grill and cook until the marshmallows are scorched, campfire style, around 2 minutes.

DESSERTS

QUEEN KILLER QUEEN OF PUDDINGS

ZZ TOP SHARP-DRESSED FLAN

SOUNDGARDEN SPOONMAN

DEAD KENNEDYS TOO DRUNK TO C**K

MÖTLEY CRÜE DR FEELGOOD'S SUNDAE

GHOST BODY AND BLOOD

RED HOT CHILLI PEPPERS BLOOD, SEX, SUGAR, MAGIK PUDDINGS

OZZY OSBOURNE BARK AT THE MOON

WHITESNAKE STILL OF THE OVERNIGHT

QUEEN

KILLER QUEEN OF PUDDINGS

Marmalade, cinnamon and star anise
mini queen of puddings

Serves 4

For the base
600ml whole milk
1 cinnamon stick
2 whole star anise
120g fresh white breadcrumbs
50g caster sugar
½ orange, juiced and zested
Butter, for greasing
2 egg yolks

For the topping
2 egg whites
4 tbsp rindless marmalade

1 Put the milk, cinnamon and star anise in a saucepan, gently bring to the boil, then take off the heat and leave to infuse for 15-20 minutes.

2 Fish out the spices then put the pan back on the heat, bring back to the boil then add the breadcrumbs, half the sugar, and the orange zest. Take off the heat then leave for 30 minutes for the breadcrumbs to swell. Meanwhile, butter 4 oven-proof ramekins.

3 Preheat the oven to 180C/375F/gas mark 5. Beat the egg yolks, stir into the breadcrumb mixture, then spread into the bottom of each ramekin and bake for about 15-20 minutes, until set.

4 Put the marmalade and 1-2 tbsp of the orange juice in a small pan and gently heat to loosen the consistency. Spread evenly over the baked breadcrumb mix in each ramekin, then set aside.

5 To make the meringue topping, put the egg whites in a clean, dry plastic bowl, then beat until stiff, gradually adding the rest of the caster sugar as you do. Spread over the puddings, creating gentle peaks. Bake again for 15 minutes, until the meringue is golden brown. Serve immediately with a jug of single cream.

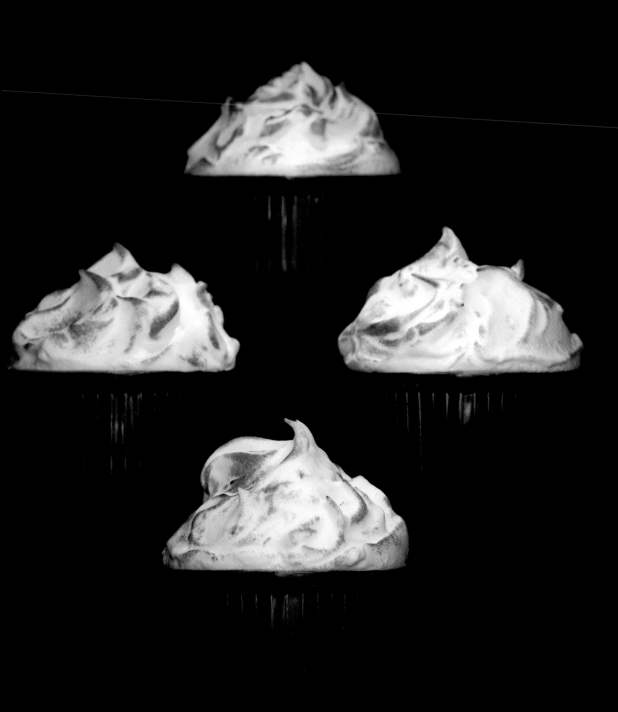

SHARP-DRESSED FLAN

Grapefruit and orange
condensed milk flan

Serves 6

For the flan
120g caster sugar
Zest of 1 pink grapefruit
Zest of 1 orange
3 eggs
**400g tin sweetened
condensed milk**
400g tin evaporated milk
1 tbsp vanilla bean paste

To serve
1 pink grapefruit, segmented
1 orange, segmented

1   Preheat the oven to 160C/350F/gas mark 3. Put the sugar and zest
in a small saucepan (it would be best to use a non non-stick pan for
this, so you can see the syrup change colour) over a medium heat,
then, without stirring, gradually melt the sugar in the pan until golden
brown, swirling every now and again to spread evenly. Take off the
heat, then pour into the base of an 18cm round glass baking dish,
making sure it is evenly spread.

2   In a mixing bowl, whisk the eggs for a minute or so, then add the
milks and vanilla, whisking again until smooth. Pour into the dish
and cover with foil.

3   Cook for around 1 hour or so, until the custard is set with a slight
wobble. Allow to cool, then invert onto a serving plate. Top with
segments of grapefruit and orange, then serve.

SOUNDGARDEN

SPOONMAN

Oreo, mascarpone and
espresso dirt cups

Serves 6

12 Oreos
2 tbsp butter, melted
8 tbsp mascarpone
8 tbsp full-fat cream cheese
3-4 tbsp cold, very strong coffee
100g icing sugar
250ml double cream, whipped to soft peaks

1 Remove the filling from the Oreos, discard, then put the biscuits into a freezer bag and crush with a rolling pin, or pulse a few times in a food processor, to rough crumbs.

2 Reserve a little of the crushed biscuits for the topping and mix the rest with the melted butter then press into the bottoms of six small glasses.

3 Beat the mascarpone with the cream cheese, then slowly mix in the cold coffee. Mix in icing sugar, tasting as you go to check the sweetness. Chill until ready to eat.

4 To serve, top with the whipped cream, and sprinkle with the reserved biscuit crumbs.

DEAD KENNEDYS

TOO DRUNK TO C**K

Ginger and lemongrass vegan cheesecake with strawberry jelly

Serves 8

For the base
16 vegan ginger oatcakes
75g dairy-free spread,
melted

For the filling
500g soya cream cheese
1 tbsp lemongrass paste
½ tbsp vanilla bean paste
200ml soya cream

For the jelly
100ml strawberry cordial
250ml water
1 sachet vege gel

1 Preheat the oven to 190C/380F/gas mark 5. Put the ginger oatcakes in a plastic bag, then finely crush with a rolling pin, or put in a food processor and pulse to fine crumbs.

2 Mix the oatcake crumbs with the dairy-free spread, then press into the base of a 20cm springform tin, to around 1cm depth. Bake for 15 minutes, until dark golden and firm. Allow to cool completely.

3 To make the filling, beat the soya cream cheese with an electric whisk until smooth, then add the lemongrass and vanilla, whisking until combined. Add the cream a little at a time, then spoon the mix into the tin and chill for 2 hours, until firm.

4 To make the jelly layer, mix the cordial with the water in a saucepan, and when warmed, sprinkle over the vege gel and stir until dissolved and the liquid has thickened. Pour over the cheesecake, then return to the fridge for another couple of hours, until set, then serve.

DR FEELGOOD'S SUNDAE

Bourbon caramel ice cream sundae with chocolate French toast and walnut brittle

Makes 6

For the sauce
300ml double cream
120g light brown sugar
2 tbsp butter
75ml bourbon

For the French toast
1 egg, beaten
100ml milk
½ tsp vanilla extract
6 chocolate chip cake bars,
or 6 slices of chocolate chip
Madeira cake, cubed
1-2 tbsp butter

For the brittle
75g walnuts, roughly chopped
A pinch of flaky sea salt
150g caster sugar

To assemble
1 large tub of vanilla ice cream

1   First, make the walnut brittle. In a large, heavy-based frying pan, gently toast the walnuts until golden, remove from the pan then set aside.

2   Mix the salt with the sugar, then tip into a small saucepan (it would be best to use a non non-stick pan for this, so you can see the syrup change colour), spreading evenly across the bottom. Heat gently, without stirring, until the sugar has turned to a golden, caramel colour. Quickly stir in the walnuts, making sure the pieces are evenly coated, then tip onto the baking tray and allow to harden. Once cool, break ⅔ into shards or bite-sized pieces, then roughly crush the rest. The brittle can be stored in an airtight container for a week or two at this point.

3   To make the bourbon sauce, put all the ingredients in a saucepan over a medium heat, then cook until the butter has melted and the mix begins to bubble. Cook for another 5 minutes, until the mixture has reduced a little, then pour into a jar. The sauce will keep in the fridge for 3-4 days.

4   To make the French toast, whisk the egg, milk and vanilla extract in a bowl. Tip the cubed cake into the bowl, making sure each piece is coated in the mix. Gently melt the butter in a frying pan, then once the butter is foaming, lift the cake cubes out of the milk with a slotted spoon, shake off the excess liquid, then fry until golden and crisp.

5   Gently warm the bourbon sauce, then divide the French toast between each bowl or sundae glass. Next, add a scoop of vanilla ice cream, drizzle over some caramel sauce, sprinkle with brittle, then repeat with two more scoops, more sauce and brittle. Top each sundae with a shard of walnut brittle.

GHOST

BODY AND BLOOD

Rye, fennel and cranberry crackers

Makes 50

200ml rapeseed oil
300ml water
4 tsp fennel seeds
50 dried cranberries, finely
chopped
2 tsp salt
2 tsp caster sugar
300g flour
300g rye flour
2 tsp baking powder

For the cordial
500g rosehips, washed
250g caster sugar

1   First, make the cordial. Put the rosehips in a large pan with 1 litre water, bring to the boil then simmer for 5 minutes. Take off the heat, allow to infuse for 30 minutes, then strain the rosehips through a muslin cloth, reserving the liquid. Put the pulp back in the pan, this time with 750ml water, and repeat the process. Repeat again with 500ml water.

2   Pour all of the rosehip liquid back into the pan, bring to the boil and reduce to around 500ml. Tip in the sugar, stir until dissolved, then pour into sterilised bottles.

3   To make the crackers, whisk the oil and water together in a large jug or bowl. Put all the other ingredients into a large bowl, add the liquid from the other bowl and mix together. Once the mixture has formed a dough, take it out of the bowl and knead on a lightly floured surface until smooth. Wrap in clingfilm then chill in the fridge for 1 hour.

4   Preheat the oven to 200C/400F/gas mark 6 and line two large baking trays with baking paper. On a lightly floured surface, roll out the dough to about ½ cm thick and cut into triangles.

5   Put the crackers on the prepared baking trays, then bake for 8-10 minutes, until golden brown. You'll need to do this in 3-4 batches.

6   Dilute the rosehip cordial with a little vodka and soda water, then serve with the crackers and a few slices of hard cheese.

RED HOT CHILLI PEPPERS

CHOC, SEX, SUGAR, MAGIK PUDDINGS

Dark chocolate and sriracha self-saucing puddings

Serves 6

For the sponge
150g self-raising flour
175g light brown sugar
50g cocoa powder
A pinch of salt
125ml milk
2 tbsp butter, melted,
plus extra for greasing
½-1 tbsp sriracha sauce
75g chocolate

For the sauce
50g dark brown sugar
1 tsp dried red chilli flakes
50g cocoa powder
450ml boiling water

1   Preheat the oven to 190C/380F/gas mark 5. Grease six large ramekins. Mix the flour, light brown sugar, salt and cocoa powder together in a large bowl, then set aside.

2   Mix the milk with the melted butter and sriracha sauce until combined, then pour into the dry ingredients and mix to a smooth batter. Melt the chocolate in a glass bowl over, but not in, a pan of simmering water, then stir through the batter and spoon into the ramekins.

3   To create the sauce, mix together the dark brown sugar, red chilli flakes and cocoa powder, then evenly sift over the pudding batter. Pour the boiling water over the mixture, using a metal spoon to make little dips for the water to seep into, then put straight into the oven and cook for around 15-20 minutes, until the crust is firm. Sift over extra cocoa powder, if you like, then serve immediately.

BARK AT THE MOON

Chocolate bark with macadamia
nuts and astronaut ice cream

Makes 8-10

75g macadamia nuts
A pinch of flaky salt
200g dark chocolate
200g milk chocolate
1 packet of astronaut
ice cream, broken into
small pieces
75g white chocolate,
roughly chopped

1 Line a 20cm x 30cm roasting tin with wax paper. Toast the macadamia nuts gently in a frying pan then remove, sprinkle with a little salt, roughly chop and set aside.

2 Melt the dark chocolate in a glass bowl over, but not in, a pan of simmering water, then pour into the base of the tin. Melt the milk chocolate in the same way, then pour over the dark chocolate. Swirl to achieve a marbled effect.

3 Scatter over the astronaut ice cream, macadamias and white chocolate, gently pushing into the chocolate base as you do so.

4 Chill for 2 hours in the fridge, or until set. Remove from the tin, then break into pieces.

WHITESNAKE

STILL OF THE OVERNIGHT

Chocolate, hazelnut and banana
chia overnight pudding

Serves 2

40g chia seeds
1 tbsp cocoa powder
250ml whole milk
2 tbsp chocolate and hazelnut
spread, plus extra to serve
50ml double cream,
lightly whipped
1 small banana, thinly sliced

1   Divide the chia seeds and cocoa between 2 glasses or jars, then
    stir to combine.

2   Pour half the milk into each, mix thoroughly, then swirl 1 tbsp of
    hazelnut spread through each glass, so ribbons of the spread run
    through the pudding, but don't mix in too much. Chill in the fridge
    overnight so the chia seeds swell up.

3   To serve, top the puddings with a spoonful of hazelnut spread,
    then some banana slices and a spoonful of whipped cream.

KITCHEN TOOLS AND EQUIPMENT

You won't need any fancy gadgetry to cook the recipes in this book, but the following are essentials in any baker's kitchen.

Brownie tins
Use a lighter metal or glass dish for these, as dark metal can make the edges too crisp, or even burnt.

Cake tins
Silverwood tins are the best in our opinion. A couple of 18cm and 20cm sandwich tins should be all you need to get started.

Bundt tins
A standard Nordic Ware tin is essential, but if you're looking to make a visual impact, you can't beat the range of bundt. If you grease these well, you'll easily avoid the mixture sticking.

Tart and pie tins
Fluted, metal and loose-bottomed are all you will need. Again, one 18cm and 20cm tin will do the trick for most things.

Loaf tins
Metal are best if well greased and lined, but silicone ones also do a good job.

Sugar thermometer
Essential for frying doughnuts. An inexpensive clip-on style one will work perfectly well.

Ice cream scoop
We've followed Martha Stewart's tip of using a scoop to ensure perfectly rounded cookies. It's definitely worth investing in one for this purpose alone.

Stand mixer
Although we have a stand mixer, these recipes are written with those that don't in mind, so directions for kneading by hand and using electric whisks are given. A stand mixer certainly makes life easier, but isn't essential.

Food processor
A mini one is ideal for grinding nuts and spices. Lakeland have really good value options.

Baking beans
A must for the pies and tarts section. Use dried kidney beans if you don't have any to hand.

Blowtorch
Not essential, but might make life prettier and more stylish for meringues, pies and puddings.

Piping bags
It's good to have a few of these, and disposable. Again, Lakeland will stock them.

SUPPLIERS

www.lakeland.co.uk
The one-stop shop for baking equipment, especially good for basics.

www.londontaxidermy.com
Home of Oliver the owl and Angus Young's horns. Thank you Alexis.

www.ebay.co.uk
Weird props, obviously....

www.medicalmodelsonline.com
Them bones, you'll find, in a number of places in this book.

www.divertimenti.co.uk
Specialist cooking shop with a good range of professional cookware.

www.cakecraftshop.co.uk
Brilliant variety of flavourings, colourings, boxes, bags and cases.

www.alansilverwood.co.uk
The best cake tins.

www.nordicbakeware.com
Great array of unusual bakeware, including spiral and cathedral bundt tins.

www.onlyfoolsandpeacocks.com
Purveyors of eclectic fancy dress.

www.daisychain.co.uk
Our go-to lady for vintage homewares.

THANK YOU

Stuart Ovenden, for the amazing photography, and belief in the project.

Kate Calder, for the sunshine you brought to every shoot day, and the incredible moral support you gave, before we even knew we needed it.

Rachel Vere for taking on the trickiest propping job ever, and making it a success. Your hard work is appreciated more than you know.

Mary Marleau - you're not just the right-hand woman, you're the backbone.

Danni Sanchez, thank you for some of the most fun times of recent years. Bake in Black would not be here without you.

A huge debt of gratitude is owed to The Flood Gallery and their amazing team for loving our crazy idea and allowing us the freedom to realise it, Tracy Sharp for design/logo/brand assistance and being the best friend/neighbour we could wish for, Bayston Road - our home from home and willing tasters, Laurence O'Reilly alongside James Nippy Blackford for editorial assistance and music consultation, Ruairi 'Bantum' Lynch, Gregor Shepherd for his keen eye and ingenious puns, Colleen and all at CAS, Drew Bradshaw for his hollow legs and drill bits, Annie B for so many things - you know what they all are, and to Fergus and Deirdre for putting on the first record.

Finally, to the Marleau, O'Sullivan, Lynch, Horsfield and Bradshaw families. This book is dedicated to you.

INDEX